# Talkin'
# Dan Gable

*Dan Gable* (signature)

# Talkin' Dan Gable

## Stephen T. Holland

Limerick Publications
Iowa City

Copyright © 1983 by Stephen T. Holland
All rights reserved. This book may not be reproduced in whole or in part without permission.
Published by Limerick Publications,
Box 2104, Iowa City, Iowa 52244.

Book Design by Andy Knoedel.
Typeset by Annie Graham & Co.

Library of Congress Catalog Card Number 83-090440

ISBN 0-9612582-0-9

Photographs by Dr. Charles Yesalis, Shyla Irving, Jeff Myers, Dave Peterson, and University of Iowa photographers.
Cover photo by Tony Triolo.

*To my Dad*
*who taught me the importance of doing my best*

# Foreword

Never before have I read a piece concerning myself where I learned so much about my personal qualities. The piece seems so true and realistic. This work has given me a more thorough understanding of myself. I have spent a lot of time thinking about what it's saying. I feel it has answered many questions concerning my life. I feel it gives special insight into why I have been so successful as a competitor and a coach. It personally has moved me on several occasions to the point of bringing tears to my eyes. These occasions usually are the ones involving my family.

I feel the writing, the way things are presented in this work, brings events in my life back fresh. It's real. It's not phony. It's like a movie, a picture being painted on the wall. With that in mind, I feel it has that much more meaning to me. It's not just a book. It sinks in and brings out what I feel are the best qualities in me, what makes me who I am.

I think that everyone should have a piece like this done on him. It makes you analyze yourself a lot more and gives your life that much more direction. It helps you understand what you've done, where you want to go.

*—Dan Gable*

# Contents

| | | |
|---|---|---|
| One | **The Match** | 5 |
| Two | **The Man Who Beat The Man** | 15 |
| Three | **A Poem For Diane** | 19 |
| Four | **View From The Top** | 27 |
| Five | **Growing Up** | 33 |
| Six | **Imagination** | 43 |
| Seven | **The World According To Garp & Gable** | 47 |
| Eight | **Red Flag Days** | 53 |
| Nine | **War Stories** | 59 |
| Ten | **Talking About Their Coach** | 63 |
| Eleven | **Days Spent Fishing** | 69 |
| Twelve | **Coaches** | 75 |
| Thirteen | **Dan Gable: Legend and Husband** | 79 |
| Fourteen | **Office Hours** | 83 |
| Fifteen | **An Ending—Because All Books Have To Have One** | 87 |

You're in a trance. You're in another world. It's just like you're on drugs. I don't know what drugs are like, but it must be something like that. Once I step into the wrestling room I change completely from one level to another. I'm gone. My body tingles. And I've got to shake all the time. All of a sudden, I've been in a state of hyperness for almost four hours. When it's done I can't get out, I'm so drained.

– Dan Gable

"*My God! Dan Gable might get beat! C'mon, Dan! Daaaaaaaan!*"

—Norm Wilkerson

Larry Owings (bottom) holds on to beat Dan Gable in the 1970 NCAA finals.

# One

# The Match

**D**an Gable sits in the bleachers following a University of Iowa wrestling practice. Leaning forward, he drops his forearms on his thighs. His hands are locked together.

It's an April afternoon, one month after Gable has coached his Iowa Hawkeyes to yet another national title. He thinks back to the last match he wrestled for Iowa State. It was the only match he ever lost in either high school or college competition. After all these years, he's still confused about how he lost. "Oh, to be honest, I don't know what the hell the scoreboard read. The crowd was yelling really loud. They didn't know what was going on. I didn't know. I wasn't thinking about losing."

**First period: Takedown, Gable. Advantage, Gable, 2-0.**

Mack Gable, a real estate salesman from Waterloo, Iowa, likes to drink a beer or two. He once was a wrestler himself. He smiles a lot. He has one of those voices that grins when he talks. He doesn't sound happy about what Larry Owings, that sophomore wrestler from the University of Washington, is saying. "I've come to beat Dan Gable," Owings vows. Bill Jauss, a sports writer for the *Chicago Daily News*, includes the quote in an article he writes. Mack reads the quote. "How dare that Owings!" thinks Mack. "Was he stupid? Dan hasn't lost since junior high — not in high school, not in college."

Because of Gable, other wrestlers flex their way out of the 142-pound weight class. Those who stay think about second place. Owings drops down two weight classes, boasting that he will defeat Gable, the man who has won 176 straight matches. Good copy for Jauss.

"If that cocky Owings keeps saying that, I'll go over and punch him," Mack thinks. "I know Dan's a better wrestler! I know it! Damn those T.V. people! Damn that *Wide World of Sports!* Why don't they leave him alone? How can he prepare mentally? He needs time! I should step in and raise hell about that! He can't wrestle that way! He needs time to psych up!"

Dan reads of Owings' boasting. "Oh, no. Not another one of those guys!" he thinks.

Owings and Gable watch each other wrestle into the finals. Gable thinks, "Owings has a good cradle, sort of sloppy, but good enough."

On their way to the final round, Owings pins four opponents and Gable five. Elapsed pin time for Owings: 16 minutes, 13 seconds. Elapsed pin time for Gable: 21 minutes, 38 seconds.

**First period: Escape, Owings. Advantage, Gable, 2-1.**

*The biggest crowd to ever watch amateur wrestling in this country is in McGaw Hall tonight, on the Northwestern campus in Evanston, Illinois. If McGaw Hall had more than 8,800 seats, more fans would have tromped through the latest Midwestern snowstorm to the gym. Gable is the attraction. Wrestling fans huddle inside—one last look at the invincible wrestler.*

*Inside, Gable is reading and screwing up cue cards for ABC, doing a promo for the meet. "Hi, I'm Dan Gable. I'm come watch me . . . shoot!" He's a "B" student, a senior in biology at Iowa State. He should be a better reader. On the 10th or 11th try, he gets it—good enough, at least, for ABC—and has a little over an hour to prepare for victim No. 182. He thinks about psyching up in the locker room. Under the bleachers, near a refreshment stand, friends wave him over. He walks over to them. They encourage him. "Tonight's the night, Danny! Go get 'em, Danny!"*

**First period: Takedown, Owings. Advantage, Owings, 3-2.**

Gable's thinking, "I'm a little scared of Owings. I'm looking for that cradle. Where's my concentration? Hey, did I get a good enough warm-up? He's got riding time on me."

**Second period: Escape, Owings. Advantage, Owings, 4-2.**

It is 1964. Gable is a sophomore at Waterloo West and has won one state wrestling title, Diane cheering him on from the sidelines. Diane, Mack and Katie Gable's only other child, is murdered that same year in the family's Waterloo home on Memorial Day weekend. Dan will win two more state titles without her.

District Court Judge Blair C. Wood sentences John Thomas Kyle, a 17-year-old, to life at hard labor, state penitentiary, Fort Madison.

Next school year, Gable puts up Diane's photo on a wall in the basement, where he works out, where he talks to Diane. "I'll always make you proud of me, Diane. I promise."

**Second period: Takedown, Owings. Advantage, Owings, 6-2.**

Norm Wilkerson, an Iowa City restaurant manager, sips at coffee that has long since lost its warmth — talking, talking, talking about Gable. "Shit, I know I could have been a national champion if he had been my coach," Wilkerson, a former Cyclone teammate, says. "He'd do anything for you. He'd sit in the damn sauna with me, even if he didn't have to lose weight. Dan would do that for everyone though, not just for me."

Fingertips tapping the table top, Wilkerson thinks back to Gable's final match at Northwestern. Talking on and on, he's in the stands in Evanston again, watching Gable, yelling for Gable, thinking about the crowd. "What a weird bunch of people. Everybody wants to see Owings win. Now it's changing. It's like, my God! Dan Gable might get beat! C'mon, Dan! Daaaaaaaan!"

**Second period: Penalty point awarded to Owings. Advantage, Owings, 7-2.**

*Gable, losing a point because of a penalty, thinks, "I ran out of bounds. I never run out of bounds. I've got to do my own thing. They penalized me a point. I've never been penalized. I'm tired. I'm not strong. I never think about being tired."*

**Second period: Reversal, Gable. Advantage, Owings, 7-4.**

In the wrestling room, Gable directs Lennie Zalesky, Iowa's 142-pounder, through a wrestling hold. Gable's hands are nondescript, not colossal, not herculean, not titanic. He pushes and pulls Zalesky's upper body back and forth with those hands. Zalesky lost to Oklahoma's Andre Metzger in the NCAA finals a year ago. The Oklahoman is again Zalesky's biggest challenge. Gable shoves his point into Zalesky, who takes a teammate to the mat the Gable way. "Way to go, stud," Gable says to Zalesky, clapping. "You just took down Metzger. Do that in the national meet."
"I can't."
"You can."

**Second period: Escape, Owings. Advantage, Owings, 8-4.**

After losing to Gable in the Olympic Trials, 7-1, Owings is talking to the winner in the showers.
"Hey, Gable, you're going to be an Olympic champion. You're going to win the Gold Medal."
"I hope so. I'd better."
"Oh, you will. Anyone who beats Larry Owings will win the Gold Medal."
Owings is a prophet. Already he has earned the only point that Gable will give up on his way to the Olympic title. From the first round of the U.S. Team Trials in Iowa City, Iowa, through his final match in the 1972 Olympic Games in Munich,

West Germany, Gable pins 12 and defeats Owings and eight others by a combined score of 130-1.

**Second period: Takedown, Gable. Advantage, Owings, 8-6.**

Dr. Adrian E. Flatt, a hand surgeon, has cast the hands of notable Americans into bronze replicas. Gable's hands are among those now in the collection, along with the hands of John F. Kennedy, John Glenn, Willie Shoemaker, Bill Russell and Dwight D. Eisenhower, to name a few. From wrists to fingertips, they are poised in a glass case on exhibit in a central walkway in The University of Iowa Hospitals. Visitors, patients, nurses, doctors and college students pause before them to measure their hands against those inside. Hand prints smear the glass case.

"Sometimes we have someone to visit in the hospital and I take the girls over." Kathy Gable, Dan's wife, is speaking. "Jenni (six years old) once was talking to her sister, Annie (four years old). 'Those are daddy's hands,' she said. There was this fellow standing there with another guy and he whispered to that guy, 'That little girl thinks those are her daddy's hands.' He didn't think we heard, but we did. And Annie hollers real loud, 'They *are* my daddy's hands!'"

**Third period: Reversal, Gable. Score tied, 8-8.**

The phone rings in Gable's office. Gable grips the receiver, wristlocking it to his ear. A man is calling from Oregon about a junior college wrestler.

"Hello?" answers Gable, as if asking a question.

"Hi, Dan. This is Larry Owings. I've got a pretty good prospect for you."

Gable wonders if Owings is serious or if he is really thinking about that match in Evanston. They pass the time.

"Okay," Gable says, "Let me know more later."
"I sure will."
Gable never hears another word from Owings about anything.

### Third period: Escape, Owings. Advantage, Owings, 9-8.

"Damn those contact lenses!" Mack thinks. "I told him he didn't need them to wrestle and now he's lost them twice. He can't even see the scoreboard."

Harold Nichols, Dan's coach, is hollering, "Get out of bounds! Get out of bounds!" Too late. Owings grabs a single leg, puts Gable on his butt and gets two points for a takedown, two more for a near-fall. "That was dumb," Gable thinks. "All I had to do was get out of bounds. But that's not my style."

### Third period: Takedown and near-fall, Owings. Escape, Gable. Advantage, Owings, 13-9.

Fifteen seconds remain. Gable has two points coming for riding time, but he doesn't know he has given up two near-fall points. He has tossed aside a troublesome contact lens. His vision is blurred. He can't see the scoreboard. He has a protective hold on Owings, keeping him away, keeping him from scoring more points. The match ends. Gable flops down on a metal folding chair. A second later, Mack is hugging his son, strongly squeezing his son's chest to his own.

Next morning, Sunday morning, *The Des Moines Register* is on the doorstep. In the sports section, *The Big Peach*, as it's called, the banner headline reads: "Dan Gable Fails."

### Winner: Owings, 13-11.

Gable is talking about Owings. "From what I understand, he's been in several different professions. Maybe he was trying to find himself. I don't know. I was reading in a newspaper once where he said, 'Beating Dan Gable was the worst thing that I ever did.' That's because he's always been known as the man who beat Dan Gable. He didn't like that. After that, everything else was anticlimactic."

Gable unlocks his hands.

*"I remember what my mother always said: 'There is never a person all that good that somebody someday can't come along and beat him.'"*

— Larry Owings

Larry Owings, as a Washington wrestler.

# Two

# The Man Who Beat The Man

As a sixth-grader in Canby, Oregon, Larry Owings' classmates called him "Porky" because Owings then packed 152 pounds on a five-foot frame. Nobody could have predicted that he would become a wrestler—and an outstanding one at that—with that sort of build. Perhaps, though, wrestling was too much in his family blood. Larry, the fifth boy in a family of seven children, had four older brothers who were wrestlers. After Larry graduated from Canby High, the Owings brothers had accounted for nine individual state championships. Larry won two of them. At the age of 17, Owings wrestled Gable for the first time, losing 13-4 in the 1968 Olympic Trials. Two years later, in the 1970 NCAA meet in Evanston, Illinois, Owings avenged that loss with a 13-11 win in the final round. From Oregon City, Oregon, where he is a high school industrial arts instructor, Owings had these thoughts about the impact of that match on his life:

> You know, nobody has called me up for about seven years out of the blue like this to talk about that match. Wrestling isn't as big out here in Oregon as it is in Iowa. Oh, I've got buddies out here who remind me of it. I went to a wedding today and a couple of old wrestling buddies of mine were there. One guy came over and said, 'There's the man who beat the man.' He also beat me once; so he said, 'And I'm the man who beat the man who beat the man.' Everybody really stresses that I was gunning for Dan Gable in that meet. A lot was made of the fact that I'd cut down two weights to wrestle him. I'd been heavier during the season, I'd wrestled at 150 and 158. Actually, though, I came up two weights. I'd wrestled at 130 in the NCAA meet the year before.
>
> I remember how loud the crowd was. I don't know if they were cheering for me, though. I was too psyched up. I was really hungry for the match. I'd

worked hard. I had the right mental attitude. I remember what my mother always said: 'There is never a person all that good that somebody someday can't come along and beat him.' I thought about that. I really accepted the challenge. I'm the type of person who works up to a challenge. The next couple of years I finished second. I'm a lot better when I have something to shoot for.

I didn't say much to him after the match. It's kind of hard to say something to someone you've just beaten. I shook his hand and wished him good luck. Later, at the awards ceremony, I clapped for him. He deserved that.

The next time I wrestled him was at the Olympic Trials. I was really trying for 136.5 pounds. The night before I was down to 138. I don't want to make excuses, but I really wasn't in a good mental frame of mind. At that time my first wife was pregnant and I didn't have a job. I also thought Dan deserved another shot at me.

I know one thing about having wrestled him. It really has made me put a little more thought into what I say. I try now to be sure what I say doesn't offend anyone. Reporters have a tendency to print some of those things. You've got to be careful.

I don't know what I would say to him if we were to talk today. I really don't. I think I'd have a tough time saying anything. It would probably be just as hard for him, though.

"Well, I was at a party, the other night,
A friendly party and we turned down the lights.
Well, after the party, I made a mistake,
I killed a good friend; now what will be my fate?
Yes, what will be my fate?
Well, I was at a party the other night,
A friendly party and we turned down the lights.
Oh, after the party I made a mistake;
I killed a good friend; now what will be my fate?
I hope they don't hang me, for what I have done.
But if the Lord wants me, then I will come.
Oh, if the Lord wants me, then I will come; Oh, I will come."

—John Thomas Kyle,
Waterloo City Jail,
June 8, 1964

Diane Gable, at age 18.

# Three
# A Poem For Diane

The phone rings at the Mack Gable Realty Co. It's June 1, Monday morning of the Memorial Day weekend. Mack has driven to a pay phone to call his Waterloo office. He's trying to reach his 19-year-old daughter Diane, who works for him as a receptionist. She hasn't answered the telephone at home and is now hours overdue for the family fishing trip on the Mississippi River near Harpers Ferry. Not Diane, but Larry McGreevey, a 23-year-old employee of Mack's, picks up the phone. Mack's order to McGreevey is, "Find Diane!" McGreevey dials a few of her friends. None have seen Diane, not in over a day. McGreevey drives to Mack's house, 2241 Easley. He checks it out. The doors are locked, the windows are locked, the garage door is down, Diane's Chevy is in the driveway, the morning newspaper is in the front door. Most alarming to McGreevey, he hears music coming from a radio inside the house. Walking to his own home, less than two blocks away, he calls Mack at the pay phone. Not Mack, but Roy Gustafson, a family friend up at the cabin for the weekend, answers the phone. Gustafson hollers across the way to Mack, who is holding his wife, Kate, in the car. Danny, their 15-year-old son, sits in the back seat.

Diane is still missing. Gustafson relates McGreevey's description of the scene to the Gables. The part about the radio with the music on alarms Mack the most. "Tell him to break in if he has to," Mack says to Gustafson.

With a piece of lumber, McGreevey smashes out a back door window. Going first to a bedroom, he finds nothing. Then, stepping into the living room, McGreevey sees Diane's body lying face up, a pair of panties and jean shorts at her feet, a sweatshirt up around her neck, the top straps of a bra torn and pulled down over her chest, teeth marks around her nose, a wound on her upper lip, her face bloodied, two stab wounds in her left breast.

McGreevey calls Harpers Ferry immediately. "She's hurt," McGreevey says. "How bad?" asks Gustafson, who listens a moment, hangs up and then walks to the car. "How bad?" asks Mack. "She's . . . not . . . alive," answers Gustafson. Screaming, Kate jumps off the car seat, running a half mile back to their cabin. Catching up with his wife at the cabin, Mack finds her banging her head on the floor. He grabs Kate, holds her. Then, without packing their clothes, without hitching up their boat, they get on the road for a two-hour drive back to Waterloo. Ten or twenty miles down the road, from the back seat, Danny says, "I think I know who did it." "You what?" asks Mack, and slams on the brakes. A few miles later, at Elkader, Mack drives to a police station. He calls the Waterloo police. "Check out Tom Kyle," he tells an officer.

* * *

It's early April. Danny Gable, 15, a state wrestling champ, is at Ahrvano's Pizza Casa with his friend Jim Bantz. Kyle's there, too, and talking about Diane, Danny's sister. Danny hears Kyle say that he would like to take Diane out and rape her someday. Danny says he'll tell Diane. Kyle says he'll do something to Danny.

* * *

Friday morning, early in the Memorial Day weekend, Kate Gable is through shopping for groceries at the Sun Mart. Kate walks to her car in the parking lot. Kyle, a boy from the neighborhood, the son of a savings and loan association president, a teen-ager who has often sat in her living room, a high school drop-out, is carrying Kate's groceries this morning. "You are going fishing over the holiday?" he asks. "Yes," Kate replies.

* * *

Tom Ogle and Dennis Jensen are playing pool on a Saturday night at the West Side Pool Hall, where they meet Kyle and John Clark. For something to do, they drive around downtown Waterloo in Ogle's Chevrolet. Kyle wants to see Diane.

They drive to her house. Diane suggests they have a party. The four boys, plus Diane, drive over to Buzz's Market on Washington Street. Diane goes in and brings back four six-packs of beer, Drewry's. She says she'll call some of her girlfriends.

Other boys—Eric Brackens, Joe Hall and Mike McLaughlin—join the party at the Gables'. Diane is on the telephone, calling girlfriends. Brenda Tomlinson, a girl Diane has known for two weeks, is on the other end of the line. Brenda has a few girls over at her house, and the idea is to get the girls together with the boys at the Gables'.

Someone notices the beer is running low. They take up a collection for more beer. Kyle goes to McGlade's Tavern. Twenty minutes later, he brings back a case of Hamm's.

Without asking Ogle, Kyle borrows his Chevrolet and goes off on his own to find Brenda and bring her to the party. A few of the other boys follow, to pick up some of the other girls. Meanwhile, Jim Lebeda, having arrived one day before from Key West, Florida, where he's been stationed at an Army base, comes to the Gable house. It's around 10:30 p.m. and he's talking to Diane. He objects to the party idea and takes Diane to McGlade's. Kyle can't find Brenda and drives back to Diane's, only to find that the party has fizzled. Then he drives to Ogle's.

At the Ogle house, Kyle phones his father and is asked to come home. It's almost 11:30 p.m. Young Kyle wants to stay longer. Around midnight, Clark and Kyle decide to see Debra Fischer on Knoll Avenue. Ogle drives them over to the Fischer house, but Debra is out on a double-date. Linda, Debra's sister, is home and Ogle drops off Clark and Kyle at the house.

* * *

Not much later, Debra arrives home. She's been out with Bill Cannon, Kenny Kohlmeyer and Doreen Funk. Cannon and Clark get into a fistfight over Debra. Kyle breaks it up. Cannon and Kohlmeyer then try to get Clark into the car. He doesn't want to go home. A neighbor woman hollers out her window to complain about the noise. They finally load Clark into the car. Cannon, Kohlmeyer, Kyle and Doreen get in, too. It's about 12:30 a.m. Clark is unloaded at Keesy's Store and walks home from there. Doreen is dropped off at her home on Mitchell Street. Kyle wants to go back to Diane's. A stop is made on Easley Street. Kyle goes to the door and is let inside the house. For two or three minutes, Cannon and Kohlmeyer wait in the car for Kyle to return. When he doesn't, they go to the front door to see if he's coming. He says no; he will walk home; they leave.

* * *

Lebeda and Diane are at the Gables' when Kyle arrives. Kyle wants to telephone Brenda. Diane gets on the phone to her first, whispers to Brenda he's drunk and tells her not to invite him over. Then Kyle gets on the phone with Brenda, who tells him it's too late and suggests he call the next day. Lebeda is about to leave. Kyle asks him for a ride to Brenda's, but Lebeda tells him it's too far out of the way. Diane says she will give Kyle a ride; she's going over to Norma Mae Gustafson's about 3 a.m., anyway. Norma Mae, who is to meet her husband Roy at the Gable cabin, couldn't get away for the holiday trip any earlier because of work. Around 1:30 a.m., Lebeda leaves. Diane promises to call him the next day.

* * *

Diane is alone with Kyle. She has to leave. She has to meet Norma Mae. Kyle should go home. She goes to the dining room in the back part of the house. She notices a window screen has been damaged and accuses Kyle. They argue. She screams and falls to the floor.

\* \* \*

The telephone rings at the Gable house. Brenda is calling. No answer. The telephone rings again. Norma Mae is calling. No answer. She keeps calling until 5 a.m., then drives to Harpers Ferry by herself.

\* \* \*

Dr. Gilbert Clark is at the Parrott and Wood Funeral Home in Waterloo, June 1. He performs an autopsy on Diane. Clark, in his opinion, says that although Diane was strangled, it was the wound to her heart that caused almost instantaneous death. Time of death: 2 a.m.

\* \* \*

Monday morning, October 5. Waterloo police detective Laverne Power is on the witness stand in John Thomas Kyle's murder trial. Kyle has already confessed to the murder of Diane Gable. Present when Kyle's confession was taken, Power is testifying about that now:
"He (Kyle) told us that after Lebeda left the house Diane was running around screaming that somebody had damaged the screen and tried to break into the house. She screamed so much he couldn't stand it; so he grabbed her around the neck and squeezed, and she went limp. In the process, some of her clothes were ripped and she fell to the floor. He thought then she was not dead and he went in the kitchen and got a brown-handled butcher knife, he called it, finally ripped·off her clothes and took the knife and stabbed her. He said he put the knife back in the kitchen, put it in a drawer and walked out the front door." Still on the witness stand, Power is telling how Kyle said he later gulped down between 50 to 60 tranquilizer pills, medication prescribed by a psychiatrist for nerves. The pills had no effect.

\* \* \*

Monday morning, October 26. Tears glistening behind his horn-rimmed glasses, 17-year-old John Thomas Kyle stands before Judge Blair C. Wood and hears himself sentenced: guilty, first-degree murder, life, hard labor, Fort Madison State Penitentiary.

Dan talks about Diane:

> I get reminded of it now and then . . . the memories come back . . . no matter how long it is . . . twenty years from now . . . things are going to come up that remind me of her. I don't think about her that much, but there are times I'm reminded of her. Like just recently my grandmother went up to her attic, brought down some mementos from when we were kids. She had a picture of Diane and me together. You open up one side . . . there's me when I was ten. You open up the other side . . . there's Diane at fourteen. It's sitting at home beside my bed now. Because it's there, I think more about her. I had even forgotten, a little bit, what she looked like. I think about . . . it brings back that vow I made to myself. Right after she died, I said, 'Hey, I'm going to make her proud. No matter what. She's going to be up there looking down and say about me, "Hey, that's my brother right there." She may not be able to be here with me, but I'm going to make it easier for her up there.'

*"You know, I've talked about winning 10 individual national championships in one year. That's kind of far-fetched. All I'd do is win that and then that would be it."*

– Dan Gable

Dan Gable, coaching.

# Four
# View From The Top

I am Dan Gable. Some say I was the greatest amateur wrestler the world has ever known. I don't know. That's for somebody else to say. Records and things never mattered to me. It's true. They didn't. You know why? Because if you let yourself think about records and winning streaks and things like that, pretty soon you've got something to defend. You don't wrestle aggressively when you're defending something.

When I was getting there, I was a lot different person. For some reason, my first two years in coaching, I didn't even think about pressure. I mean, I was into it, but I was only the assistant, and I didn't think about it. Like in practice, I went to practice and I tried to get the guys to improve. I explained a lot of things to them that I thought they could do better. I got disappointed at times when they didn't do them on the mat. But yet, at the same time, I never thought about pressure.

As we won, sure there's more pressure now. But then again, I'm confident instead of feeling pressure, if you can figure those two things out. If I was pressured to the point where I felt, 'We've got to win, we've got to win,' I'd have a hard time doing it. I'd probably be in the nuthouse. But I'm confident I've got the program established and the kids are doing the things they're supposed to do to win. What I'm saying is that it was probably harder to get the program up. A lot of people say, 'It's rougher to keep it on top.' I don't think so. You've got the atmosphere developed.

Now everybody is looking at us. They don't like to see us win all the time. Like, in 1978, in Maryland, we won the NCAA title. It was my first title as coach. I can remember how a lot of coaches came up to me and said, 'Congratulations.' It was an honor for me. A lot of coaches felt, 'He has never won it. It's good for him.' In 1979, we won the national title for the second time. We walked away with it and very few coaches said anything to me. In 1980, when we won it again, I don't think any coaches congratulated me. They were happy for me once. But it's come to the point now where they despise me. The more you win, the more people despise and want to beat you.

So what I'm saying is that the more you win, the more you concentrate on winning, the more you hurt people. Not necessarily hurt people, but get people upset. Either you're hurting people or getting them upset at you. But, hey, that's fine. The one thing that motivates me more than anything else is winning.

You know, I've talked about winning 10 individual national championships in one year. That's kind of far-fetched. All I'd do is win that and then that would be it. My goal is to win as much as I possibly can. At the same time, besides winning, I want the athletes to leave here with good feelings and being stable people.

I don't see myself being the wrestling coach forever. I don't see it. For some reason, I can only look into the immediate future. I don't even know what I could do if I didn't coach. I don't think I want to be an athletic director. I know I don't want to teach. And yet, I don't think I want to coach for that long, either. I think I'll coach for as long as I'm effective. I don't know how long a man can keep up this kind of competition. That's all I'm saying. I mean, when I start not putting my whole heart into it so that we end up not doing as well as we should, then it's time to put someone else in there who wants to put in the time and effort.

I'm not saying I don't put my whole heart into it because I could be doing a lot more than I even do. But then I probably wouldn't be married. I'd be divorced. I mean, you've got to have priorities. You look back at your own career and you say, 'Well, I did this. I did that. I'm dedicated.' I look back and see I could have been more dedicated. But then maybe I would have been worse off. Because, maybe, you've got to have things to divert yourself with. I don't think anybody can be 100 per cent straight. You've got to have releases.

What's next? That's a tough one! It really is. I try to figure out what I would do if I didn't wrestle. But I can't think of anything else. I've gotten so much satisfaction out of what I'm doing. It's hard to make the break. But I can't think about ten years from now. It would put too much mental strain on me. The way I coach, if I thought I had to do this for ten more years, I wouldn't be able to do it. I have to do it now, at the time. So right now, I really don't have any long-range goals. I talk about building a new house. That's my next real goal. Right now I'm happy being Dan Gable. Whatever that means. I think about what I am, though, and what I might do, at times.

"*He* was a patrol boy, good student and always was vice-president or president of his room in school. He majored in biology and history in college. He had a lot of interests, but, you know, he couldn't plant a carrot."

— Katie Gable, mother of Dan

Dan Gable, as a high school sophomore.

# Five
# Growing Up

**A**sk about her son, Dan, and Katie Gable's eyes widen, yet it's not easy to gaze into them. She flits and flutters between the living room and the kitchen of her Waterloo home, not saying much. Slighter these days, more frail because of her struggle with cancer, Katie, when she is in the living room, perches on the edge of a straight-back chair. "Oh, you don't want to hear me," she says. "Mack can tell you more than I can."

Katie is off again, appearing minutes later with a scrapbook, a thick one, bound in red, its pages darkened by the years. "This is one of the scrapbooks we made for Danny," she says, flopping it down with a thump on the coffee table. "That'll tell you about Danny."

As she thumbs through it, the pages of ink and photos flip past, telling, but not the way a mother can, about her son. She caresses the bound pages to her bosom, one end of the book resting on her thighs. She sits farther back on the straight-back chair, but not all the way back, rocking herself with memories. For a while, she talks of Dan, but it's obvious she'd rather show off memorabilia throughout the house.

Setting the cumbersome scrapbook back on the coffee table, she's now a tour guide. Mack follows her. Dan's Olympic Gold Medal is on a living room wall, next to a picture of Diane. Down a hallway is Dan's boyhood room, overflowing with artist sketches, ribbons, medals and articles about him. "When Dan comes home with Kathy and the girls, they all sleep here," she says.

In the basement of the house is the wrestling workshop. Katie points to the main attraction. "There's the mat he used," she says. The mat's smallness is overwhelming – it looks right for a junior high wrestler but hardly big enough for an Olympic champion.

The small mat, Mack explains, taught his son to stay in the middle, the place to score points. "There's the bike," Katie continues, adding that Dan wore out two of those machines.

Then she points to a small set of weights. "And those are the very weights he used."

A too-small mat, too few weights and overworked bike machines: How could this add up to an Olympic champion? Katie says it was through love and hard work.

> I've got all his Valentine's Day cards downstairs, and Christmas cards, you know. How could I tell you what they mean to me? Oh, they're full of 'to mother,' and 'how wonderful you are,' you know. And he gave me my own trophy in junior high, him with all of his, and all. It's about two inches high, up there on the mantel. Says 'World's Greatest Mom.'
>
> Every weekend from college, here'd come his friends from Ames. Of course, we'd love to have them all. They'd come home, bring all their dirty clothes. We'd spend all weekend just getting their stuff done for them. Cook all day, too. It didn't matter what we cooked. They'd eat it all anyway. The boys really appreciated it. A lot of them were from out-of-state, you know. Didn't have no one to do those things for them.
>
> When he lost that last college match I was heartsick. Boy, that was bad! He was so sad, Dan was, that anyone that was around him was just automatically sad. Oh, he was really down and sad. I think, after a couple of days, he started to work even harder, though.
>
> Three months before the Olympics, all he did was run, run, run; work, work, work; wrestle, wrestle, wrestle. But the hard work paid off. He came home with the Gold. If he hadn't, that other loss would have been nothing, compared to this.
>
> But I never doubted Dan.

\* \* \*

Growing Up

Born: Mr. and Mrs. Mack Gable, 1647 W. 11th, a boy at Allen Memorial.
— *Waterloo Daily Courier,* October 25, 1948

Dan Gable is waiting at a pizza place. Sliding off his bar stool, a mug of beer in his hand, he's ready to be interviewed. Worried about his time schedule, he steps quickly to the table. "I only have until seven-thirty, tonight," he says, sliding into the booth. "I've got to see the kids and pick up Kathy. We've got a meeting at eight. That's about an hour. Is that enough time? If not, get me later." Sausage and mushroom pizza is on order. Dan talks, taking himself back to when he was a youngster growing up in Waterloo, Iowa.

>Childhood moments? For some reason, as a young kid, I was pretty ornery. I don't know why. I don't remember a lot of the early things I did. They were just told to me. But I was, uh, a very belligerent kid. I can remember growing up. My mom used to break rulers over me all of the time. I used to eat more soap than food. My dad had a ring. He would either spank me over his knee or crack me on the head with that ring. Maybe that's why I'm so goofy. I don't know.
>
>Once I was getting on an elevator with my mom in a Waterloo department store. There was a whole bunch of people in there. And in those days you didn't have an automatic button. You had a guy who was the elevator man. And I guess I was trying out some new words. I looked up at him and said, 'Fifth floor, you bastard.' So my mom acted like she didn't even know me. So when the elevator stopped on the next floor, she got out and left me there. So I started screaming and running after her.
>
>In that same episode at that department store, my mom and I were walking around and some fat lady

**36 Talkin Dan Gable**

was bent over looking at something. I walked right up behind her and took a big ol' bite right out of her butt.

And another time, for some reason I hated to go to the barber shop. So I tricked my mom. What happened was my mom would take me to the barber shop. I figured when she stopped the car to park I'd be real calm and cool. I waited until she got out and started plugging the meter. Then I crawled over and locked her car door. She'd left the keys inside. And I locked her side and I locked mine and I sat inside that car for an hour. She couldn't get in to get me and I wouldn't get out. I didn't have to get a haircut, but, of course, I only got away with that once.

Then another thing. My big thing was this convertible. And, uh, my big thing was throwing stuff out of the car. Whenever the top was down, whatever was in the car, I'd throw out. I used to throw my mom's purse out a lot. Then my parents would have to go back and pick it up.

I can remember in grade school I had a friend, Billy Baptist. To this day he could tell you about the time I tied up his hands with wire and drugged him home from school. Wait a minute; that was the neighborhood kid next door. No, he was the policeman's kid. I'm getting a couple mixed up. I think the policeman's kid came over bragging about his father's police car. I think I only beat his head against a telephone pole. Well, anyway, one of them I drugged home from school. If he fell down, I'd pull him along the ground.

I got in trouble a lot. Once I chased this cat across the roof of a neighbor's garage. I was in grade school. First, second, third grade. Once I got up there the cat jumped off. So I didn't get the cat. But I pulled about 100 shingles off the roof. I ripped them off and threw them on the ground. Of course, the people who lived there saw me and told my dad. I got a crack on the head with his ring.

Another time, on a Saturday, these construction people were building houses. Of course, construction people don't work on Saturdays. But I used to play in amongst the houses that were being built. They were getting ready to put up a brick front. They had all kinds of stacks of bricks. And I took the bricks, and they had this concrete basement poured and already hardened. Well, I took those bricks and I threw them down from up above and broke them all. I did a whole bunch of damage. I can remember my dad being there when the construction man came. He put me right over his knee and beat my butt. I mean, he beat it good. Then he cracked me over the head with his ring. I got them both, a butt spanking and a crack over the head with the ring. That hurt. I mean, it hurt good.

I'd never swear at my dad. But in front of my mom, yeah. I can remember one time we were getting into the car and I yelled real loud, 'You bitch!' I could see the look on her face. Boy, I'll tell you, I knew what was going to happen to me. She was going to tell my dad, which she did. I knew I was going to be in trouble. Once she told him, immediately, I'd be hitting the ground. A couple of hours and her being mad would wear off and it wouldn't be so bad. So that was one of the times I ran away. I used to run away a lot. At least once a week. I had a Boy Scout pack. I was a Cub Scout for a little while. I made my Bear. No, wait a minute. What do you have? Cub, Bear, Lion? Yeah, what's the lowest? Cub? I guess it's Cub. I made my Cub and had to pull out. Anyway, I'd take that pack and fill it full of clothes. I'd run away from home. I'd never stay gone more than an hour, ever. I did that several times. In fact, we've got home movies of me leaving.

One incident, which sticks in my mind, was when I was three, maybe it was four. I hadn't learned how to swim yet. I always would be around construction, like I said. The street people were digging for a pipe. They had a big, deep hole, about eight feet deep. It rained and the hole was full of water. I fell in that hole and I almost drowned. I can remember it scared the hell out of me. My folks just reprimanded me for playing around the construction site. Crack, the ring over my head.

Sometimes I did things just for the laugh, I guess. Like one time we'd gone to the Dairy Queen and I was eating a soft ice cream cone. My dad and I got into an argument. So I took that ice cream cone and smashed it against the back of his head. And it just stuck there. Boy, did I catch hell!

My dad would take me to University of Iowa football games and to major league baseball parks, and I'd always pack my pea-shooter. We'd go into Chicago or to Iowa City and I'd sneak around in between cars and shoot peas off the windows. I loved it when the window was open. I loved parades. Parades were my big thing. I'd fire those peas off the heads of horses.

My best friends, in junior high, were the biggest hell-raisers. Not hoods. They were the kind who would ring doorbells, throw eggs at cars. Our big thing was tipping over garbage cans. We used to do that stuff constantly. But once I got into high school, I got into wrestling and I wasn't quite so ornery. I didn't go out that much, except maybe a little bit in the spring.

\* \* \*

Mack Gable is sitting in his kitchen, telling about the night he organized a plane trip to Oklahoma. One of his pals thought up the idea. Dan, Mack's unbeatable son, was to wrestle in a state known for its wrestling champions. A few more Iowa voices could help.

"It'll cost three or four hundred dollars," Mack told his buddies, after checking with a charter service. "Get 10 or 12 guys. That's not bad."

Names went down on the count-me-in list. Fly into Oklahoma, cheer for Dan and fly back to Waterloo the same day. The day of the meet, Mack packed a six-pack or two—flight fuel. But during the course of the day the telephone rang and the excuses came, until only Mack was left.

"What could I do?" he asked. "I'd already promised the kid." As the only passenger, Mack flew in and out of Oklahoma, picking up the entire tab. It was a short match. Dan pinned his opponent in the first period.

> Do you want me to tell you when I thought he was really, really tough?
>
> It wasn't in high school. I was there for every match. I never missed an out-of-town match or anything. He won those three state titles. He didn't have much of a problem winning them. Well, I shouldn't say it that way, sounds kind of cocky or something. He had some tough matches, but he never wrestled a kid in high school I wasn't confident he could beat.
>
> It was when he was a freshman at Iowa State, and when he went to the Midlands Tournament and he beat Masaaki Hata (1962 NCAA champion for Oklahoma State and two-time Midlands champion). It was unbelievable. I was surprised. Yeah, I really was. I knew the kid was a good wrestler, but he was a freshman beating national champions. I couldn't see how he could ever get beat after that.
>
> There was that time he went up a weight and wrestled Mike Grant. You know, the guy who was the NCAA champion at Oklahoma? I thought it was a crazy thing

to do. It was just goofy, but his teammates down at Iowa State were ribbing him and talking him into doing it. The coach (Harold Nichols) didn't want him to do it. Well, he wouldn't have done it if he didn't want to, but these guys persuaded him into it. He won, but I still think he shouldn't have done it.

You know, in the Olympics he got hit in the head in the first period of his first match. The kid came out and butted him and the eye popped open and squirted blood all over everything. So, anyway, they went out and greased him up, put some stuff on there to stop the blood, bandaged it. And then one of the damn foreign referees said he couldn't put that kind of stuff on it. They had to put some kind of resin on it. They had to stop the match again. Hell, three more seconds on the time-out clock and he would have been disqualified.

When he won that Olympic Gold Medal, they played *The Star-Spangled Banner* and he kissed that medal. He wasn't that kind of a guy. That was from the bottom of his heart.

You know, I probably get more credit for it all than I deserve. He wasn't hard to push. No, I didn't push him at all. He was self-dedicated and he did it. He was an easy kid to raise. Like, for instance, there was this one time when I went over to one of his practices at the high school and he told me to get out. Said I was messing him up. Hell, I wasn't going to mess up the kid. Then he gave me this picture. I've still got it. On the back he wrote: 'Dad, I'm really proud to have a dad like you and I hope to stay as proud in the future. You can watch me wrestle anytime. Love, Danny.'

"*The* big thing about me that is unbelievable is my imagination. My imagination is unbelievable."

– Dan Gable

In 1961, Dan Gable and his Reds teammates won the Optimists' city title. Mack is in back (second from right). Dan is in front (third from right).

# Six

# Imagination

**W**hat motivated him? About Dan Gable, many say he was motivated to win the Olympic title because of his sister's murder. Others say that's not all there was to his motivation. A favorite line about Gable is, "He just wanted to be the best." But neither wanting to be the best nor being driven by the lost love of a sister could ever have been—even together—enough. To achieve an Olympic title, you have to find a way to make the dream a reality. For Gable, his imagination was the key.

> When I was growing up, Bob Richards, the Olympic champion, came to our school. He told us what we had to do to become an Olympic champion. A lot of people said that sounded good, but I actually believed him and did them.
> The big thing about me that is unbelievable is my imagination. My imagination is unbelievable. Everything I did, it was like I was really there. Starting in grade school, I followed all of the sports. I would either play with that team in mind or play against that team. Of course, I was always playing for or against the Yankees. I'd play with the kids after school and then bring them home, in my imagination, and play after supper. We'd always be playing in the World Series. Of course, whoever had me always won. I'd be talking to myself, standing there in our front yard, cars driving by, a bare spot on the left and right where I stood, striking out the side. We had a bush. It was about a three-foot evergreen. That was the catcher.
> In the winter, I'd play football in the front room. I'd have all of the chairs and couches all lined up like defensive players. Then I'd run into them, bounce off of them, spin, after taking the tailback hand-off. I'd do this for hours.
> Swimming was another big one. When I wasn't

making baskets through a fake hoop, swish, in my basement, I'd be swimming across it. I'd do every kind of stroke for hours. I'd walk back and forth, swimming with my arms. I'd hit the walls, do a flip turn and swim back the other way.

I loved fishing. I'd put my waders on and go out in the yard. We had a boat and a folding cot and I'd sit there, put my stringer out and fish. Whatever sport I liked, I'd spend hours and hours imagining it, catching fish, hitting home runs and scoring touchdowns. I hit so many home runs, caught so many fish and scored so many touchdowns. The thing was that it was so real to me. It felt like it was actually going on. Later, in junior high school, I began doing this with wrestling.

People who shoot off their mouths a lot I've always had as heroes. I like Muhammad Ali. I like Reggie Jackson. I know him personally. I guess my whole life has been like that. My heroes right now, if I get a chance to watch, are the Russian wrestlers. I look to people who excel. Before, in my life, it was all kinds of people. Now it's narrow, defined. I specialize. I'm ignorant of a lot of things in the world. I give a lot of responsibilities to my wife. I let my lawyer do a lot of things because I don't even want to know. I don't read newspapers. It hurts me because there are so many bad things going on. I pick up the newspapers and there's deaths, volcanoes, tornadoes, air raids, killings, fighting in other countries and bombs. Why do I want to bog down my mind with all of that stuff? I've got positive things I want to do.

"*When Dan Gable lays his hands on you, you are in touch with grace.*"

—John Irving,
 *Esquire* magazine
 April 1973

Author John Irving, as photographed for the cover of *Time* Magazine.

# Seven

# The World According To Garp & Gable

**I**n each other's domain, John Irving and Dan Gable admit they are uncomfortable. They respect each other's abilities and share a common interest in the sport of wrestling. Irving, best known as the author of *The World According to Garp*, uses wrestling metaphors throughout his writing. Irving is a former collegiate and AAU wrestler. He often takes breaks from his writing by wrestling with his three sons. While at the University of Iowa's Writers Workshop in the early '70s, Irving often worked out with Gable and the Hawkeye wrestlers.

In an article Irving wrote for *Esquire* magazine on Gable, entitled "Gorgeous Dan," he tells of the night he went with the Olympian to a high school football banquet in Solon, Iowa. After Gable gave a speech and showed off his Olympic Gold Medal, a teenage waitress asked Irving for an autograph. He writes: "I don't mistake for a minute that it's because she's read one of my novels. It's because I came in with him. 'I'm not even famous,' I tell her. In tone with the optimism of Gable's speech, she tells me, comfortingly, 'Well, maybe someday you will be!'"

Irving on Gable:

> By the time I met Dan, my really active wrestling was over. I mean, I was much more of a writer than I was a wrestler, but I found him a wonderful inspiration. He meant a lot to me the first time I got together with him in 1973 or '74. But I haven't really kept in contact with Dan since I left Iowa in 1975. I sometimes keep in contact with J Robinson, his assistant. I'm not really close to Dan. I don't think it's fair to say I'm close to Dan, but he's a special person to me, a hero of mine. You can't be around him without noticing his intensity. I think the only models that anyone has ever had or are worthwhile are people who do something with intensity. In recent years, any models that I've had have come out of books, out of literature, not athletically.

Gable is a pure spirit, not to be confused with a free one. He's like anyone who is devoted to something, no matter what the cost.

Dan is never satisfied. There are a lot of wrestlers who feel that if you get a good single leg, and you get a couple of good upper body moves, and you can ride well, and you have a good escape move from the bottom, that's all you need. And you just sort of work on these things. Well, Dan is the athlete's equivalent of the Renaissance man. It is not enough for him to learn how to do one thing, and that gives him a tremendous amount of confidence. It means that if you meet somebody for whom your one good ride doesn't work, you know more than one. And the triplicate of it is that he is a very determined man. People who are good teachers are usually good students. That is, they are interested in the whole process. He must never as a young wrestler have been satisfied or complacent with getting good at a certain number of moves. Anything he didn't know about he was curious about. He is that way as a coach, too. If he sees that you don't know about something, he wants you to know about it.

There are a lot of people who can demonstrate moves. It is unquestionable the guy has more authority because you know what he's done. But I think he's a good teacher or a good coach as well because he seems to pay a great deal of attention to what you do. So much has been made of Dan as the wrestler, as sort of a super conditioner, super physical in wrestling, which of course is what he is capable of being. He was in super condition, and he was capable of being physical with anybody, but I always thought that his strength in wrestling was to be able to capitalize on his opponent's weakness. Certainly, that's his strength as a coach, too. He can look at you and know what is wrong with you.

I wasn't in the greatest of shape when I wrestled Dan, but I always liked working with him because he was such a marvel. He could always show you something. He had an impact on me, you understand, not because I was interested any more in wrestling, but because I was interested in working at the best of my ability. I realized I wasn't doing it.

Gable on Irving:

As for John Irving, I think he just showed up on the mat one day. I'm not really sure. He was just a guy who wanted to work out with me. I thought, 'What the heck? I'll give him a workout.' And he came back. And I respect him for that. I respect him just because he wanted to come and get a workout for physical fitness.

He must be a helluva writer. He went with me one night to a speech I gave at Solon High School. He did a story on me for *Esquire* magazine. Called it 'Gorgeous Dan.' He said, 'I want to go with you one night. That's all.' He really caught me in that one night. If I ran my hand along a car hood a certain way, he had it in there. But that's all I ever read of his.

He had me over for supper one night. I couldn't believe I accepted. But I did. I went over to the house. To be honest, I was freaked out. I mean, when I went into this house, I felt like I was in a foreign country. I guess it was the atmosphere or the way they talked. Of course, they were from out East somewhere. Anyway, the house was different. I just felt I was around a lot of people who were, well, kind of weird. But that doesn't mean anything. That was one time.

*"This is the hardest working team I've ever seen. These workouts are intense."*

— Dave Ash, student trainer

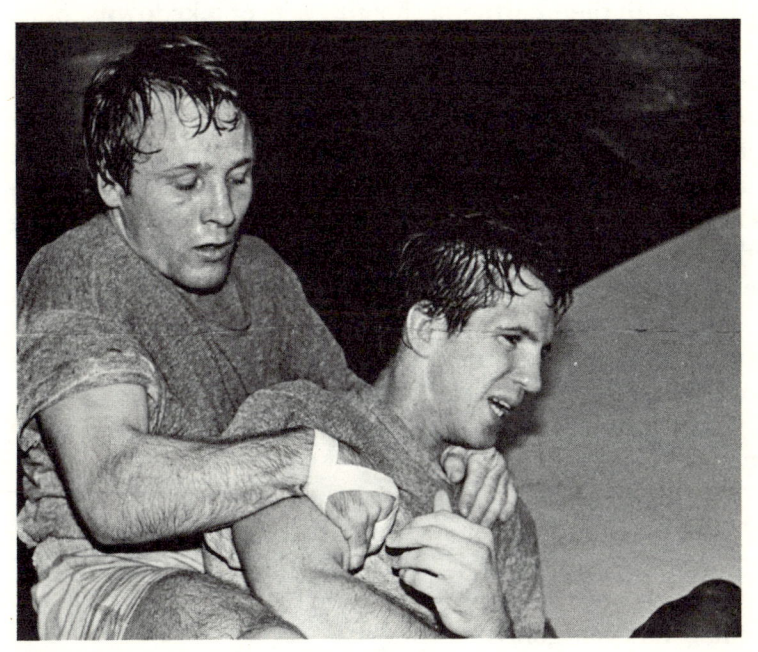

Hawkeyes Barry Davis (left) and Tim Riley at practice.

# Eight

# Red Flag Days

**R**ed Flag Days come three or four times a year. They're days when Iowa mat coach Dan Gable is hard-hearted, days of sweat-drenched bodies, days when waterbreaks last 20 seconds.

Before their first drink, the wrestlers slide on pools of sweat, drilling with their partners, shooting sets of takedowns, practicing escapes. Fifteen minutes into the afternoon workout, they get their first break. They sprint to the water cooler at the far end of the room and swig down Squinch. Briefly they relax, then sprint back to their slippery places on the mat.

Dave Fitzgerald, Iowa's top 167-pounder, takes a rest. Fitzgerald knows better than to lie on his back. It's against the rules. But he's worked hard. All he wants is a few more seconds of rest. Sorry, Fitz.

"Fitzgerald, what are you doing?" Gable asks, more as a command than a question. Dizzy, pulling himself up on one knee, Fitzgerald says, "I can't breathe."

"What do you mean you can't breathe? Fitzgerald, what happens when you can't breathe?"

"You die."

"You're right! You die! Are you dead, Fitzgerald?"

"No."

"You can breathe then! So get going!"

Fitzgerald gets going.

Filling the paper cups with Squinch, which tastes like unsugared Kool-Aid, Dave Ash, a sophomore student trainer, watches, shaking his head at the sight in front of him. "This is the hardest working team I've ever seen," Ash tells a visitor while handing him a cup of the liquid to keep him cool. "These workouts are intense."

The Squinch is ready. Gable hollers to his wrestlers, "Okay, break!" But the action doesn't stop. It just slows down. Drinking on the run, they spill more Squinch on themselves than they gulp down. Gable keeps count, "You've got to the count of 10 to get back to your stations. One, two, three, four . . ."

The wrestlers run back to sweat some more.

While picking up the dropped cups, Ash feels a draft—a cool breeze in this room of stench. Hey, that's not good! There's not to be a breeze. Heat is the wrestler's joy. Heat is the way to lose weight, to get into shape. Ash sees the door slightly open. He walks over and shuts it. There's no more breeze. The wrestlers are sweating so much that the mat shines with perspiration. Balance is hard to keep, the mats are so slick. The short squeaking sounds of wrestling shoes turn to long, sliding squishes on the wet surface. The sounds of slippery bodies slap against each other, echoing off the walls. This isn't pretty. It's downright ugly.

* * *

Sitting in his street-side office, the one with the plants growing in upside-down Hawkeye football helmets, Gary Kurdelmeyer talks about the idea behind Red Flag Days. He came to the University of Iowa in 1967—a big, dumb kid from Cresco, he calls himself. He started Red Flag Days when he was the coach. He's a former wrestler, an NCAA champion. He has coached two NCAA championship teams and is now an assistant athletic director. When he was the coach, he wanted to test his wrestlers, to break them, to bring out their raw instincts. He told them it wasn't punishment. It was to test them, to see if they could reach down inside themselves to find something more.

* * *

Gable doesn't want his wrestlers to know when to expect a Red Flag Day. He wants to keep it in the back of their minds, to make them fear it.

"It's a psychological thing," he explains. "They fear it but they realize they can do it."

The coach is thinking about making the days harder, thinking about going to a higher level of pain, inventing a new day—Black Flag Day.

"That might wipe my guys out," he says, of his bigger plans for pain, "like that bug spray Black Flag does to insects."

Wearing a baggy, yellow Hawkeye sweatshirt and gray sweat pants, Gable watches his wrestlers. Casually, he adjusts his glasses.

"A couple of you guys are letting up," he shouts. But most of them are hanging in there. The practice will last 80 minutes. Gable says that's all a human being — even one of his wrestlers — can push himself. He moves to the center of the room — time to push.

"I don't think we can make an hour," he says. "C'mon, studs! Love it! Love it! Love it!"

One wrestler pleads for rest.

"I'm tired!" he says.

"Keep going!" Gable answers.

The wrestler keeps going.

The last 10 minutes are the most intense. Gable encourages more, talks more, claps his hands harder. The wrestlers respond. Leg lifts are done with more groaning. Then partners lock arms and bang chests, beads of sweat flying in all directions. Ten sprints around the room, one for each weight, led by the starter at each weight, end the workout.

Cheers from the wrestlers, comrades of shared pain. They clap for themselves, for each other. Wet, gray T-shirts are peeled off and dangled at the wrestlers' sides. Gable is clapping harder now, telling them to jog a few laps, to cool down slowly. They jog two, three laps. Gable orders a halt and waves them into the center of the room, close to him. Stumbling into each other, some weaving on unsteady legs, the wrestlers hear Gable.

"Hey, some of you broke verbally today," Gable says, talking about the swearing he had heard. "But not one of you broke mentally. There's not a bunch of athletes or a sports team anywhere that went through what we went through today. I'm proud of you."

The wrestlers cheer, their yelling and clapping drowning out the sounds of Gable's voice and hands.

"*Kids come here today because they want to be close to him. They want to get some of that mystique rubbed off on them. I think that's probably why I'm here, too. That's probably why everybody is here.*"

— Bob Lowe

In the 1983 Big Ten meet, Iowa won 9 of the 10 individual championships.

# Nine

# War Stories

**B**ob Lowe, twice Amateur Wrestling Coach of the Year in Canada, recently received his M.A. degree in sports psychology from the University of Iowa. One day he was teasing Dan Gable. "Hey, Dan Gable, you're pretty big stuff," Lowe says. "How'd you get to be so big?"

Without saying a word, Gable hands Lowe a book, *Dan Gable: The Wrestler*, written by Russ L. Smith of the *Waterloo Courier*. Reading it that night, Lowe learns about the murder of Diane, Gable's sister, and Dan's vow to always get the best out of himself.

The next day Lowe returns the book to Gable. Gable takes it from him and writes in it, "To Bob Lowe — if you learn as much from me as I've learned from you, we'll both benefit from our relationship." He gives the book back to Lowe. "Fantastic," thinks Lowe, "but what can he learn from me?"

Lowe on Gable:

> His organization in practice is really something. Like he has these war stories. Well, the week before the national meet he'll tell them. They're designed to motivate the wrestlers. He tells stories about past national champions and some of the adversities they went through. Like there was this Japanese guy in '69 who won the World Championship. He had a dislocated shoulder, his arm hanging out, and he went on to beat the Russian. And guys making weight? He tells stories about Rick Sanders, a big wrestling name, was at the World Championships in England and he lost 25 pounds in one night to make weight.
>
> He acts out these stories himself. He talks and everybody sits in a circle. It's kind of out of character for him. So they're more effective. He will have guys carrying him across the mat like Rick Sanders who couldn't make weight. He's too weak but he's got to get to the

scales. He's lying on the floor, breathing under the door like he's in the sauna, all the time pretending he's Rick Sanders.

It's kind of funny, and they do motivate the wrestlers. They're designed to show no matter how you feel in a situation, there have been guys who have felt worse. It can really help when it's the end of the season and you're cutting weight.

In practice, he barely says anything, when he's not doing the war stories. Dan never has to say something 100 times. He knows it's just the way it's said or the time that you say it—that's more important. If I hear the same thing 100 times, pretty soon it doesn't mean much any more. But if it comes at you one time—at the right time—it sticks to you. It's the same thing with his encouragement. He doesn't come right out and say 'Hey, you're doing a helluva job.' But every once in a while he says something that will drive you until the next time he says something. Hell, the guy is a legend. He is something and it means a lot if he says anything. It wouldn't mean as much if he said it all of the time.

It will be interesting to see 10 years down the pike if he is just as effective a coach as he is now. Kids come here today because they want to be close to him. They want to get some of that mystique rubbed off on them. I think that's probably why I'm here, too. That's probably why everybody is here.

"*This* may sound weird, but I believe when he gets really tired that psychs him up. When he gets tired he gets more energy and he wants to wrestle harder. It sounds weird, but the more I watch the man, the more I think that's the case."

— Ed Banach

Twins Ed (left) and Lou Banach.

## Ten

# Talking About Their Coach

Lou Banach, a former Iowa heavyweight wrestler, a two-time NCAA champion, watches the Hawkeye baseball team clobber a small college team from in-state. Sitting in the stands behind home plate, he talks about the differences between himself and his coach, Dan Gable.

"A lot of guys come here as freshmen and they want to do everything he did," he says. "These guys come here and they go out thinking just like him. Well, I have my own thoughts. People may think I'm flaky, and that's okay. I want them to think I'm flaky. It helps in wrestling. People don't know what to expect that way."

During his sophomore year, Banach quit the team but returned the following year. He talks about how Gable handled the situation:

> Dan is the kind of person who understands. He didn't totally separate himself from me as a person. He looked at me as a wrestler and said, 'Okay, maybe you're not making the right decision.' But I quit the team and he looked at me as a person who was trying to work out his problems and was happy with what I was doing. He said, 'Okay, you think you know what you want for yourself. I can't really down you for that.' He let me go. He cut the strings. But in the back of his mind he knew that I would come back. That was a nice part about Dan. He didn't give up on me. He would see me in the locker room and he would come up and talk to me. He was always a friend to me. It's hard to imagine how in the times that were so frustrating and with the hardships that had occurred between the two of us that we began to really become friends. It scarred both of us pretty badly and we came closer out of it. It seemed like I helped him a little bit to become a better coach and he helped me become a better wrestler and a better person.

\* \* \*

Watching his twin brother Lou wrestle Gable in practice one afternoon, Ed Banach, a three-time NCAA champion, saw how tired they were becoming. "Break?" Gable asks Lou, a one-word request. "Okay," Lou grants. While Lou lies on his back, Gable goes to the water cooler to rinse off and then walks back to the spot where his wrestling partner is a wet blob in a puddle of sweat. The trip takes less than a minute. "Want to wrestle some more?" Gable asks Lou. "Okay," Lou says. Ed is still watching, thinking, "He's fresh. Gable is fresh. Lou is dead tired and Gable is fresh. It's weird. The more tired Gable gets, it seems the more fresh he is. He gets tired and he wants to wrestle harder. Dan Gable gets a lot of pleasure out of working his body really hard."

Ed Banach on Gable:

> Wrestling him makes you more aware of your feelings. When you wrestle you have a sense of weight, a sense of force, a sense of balance. Other people let you get away with leaning on them, not Gable. He's so far ahead of everyone else. He's a combination of all the best wrestlers in the room. He's like Bruce Kinseth. He's coming after you. He's like my brother Louie. When he gets thrown he's right up on his hips again. He's like Mike DeAnna. He's really quick, fluid and smooth. You can have him where you think you've got him dead cold and he's not going to do anything. All you have to do is wait for him to make one move and you're going to throw him on his head. But then he makes that one move and the next thing you know you're on your back. What happened? He's like J Robinson. He's got really, really good technique. He's a combination of all these guys. But yet, he's the best at every one of those things. He can throw you

like I throw you; he can shoot on you like Chuck Yagla shoots on you. He can do anything and everything anybody can do. So he's a master of everything. I mean, that's the amazing thing about him.

He teaches by example, by imagery, by feeling. He will say, 'Well, get here and get there. When you're here you will do that and you'll feel where you're going. This is how you will shoot back.' What do you do? You form a picture in your mind. So he'll say, 'Instead of pushing through the man, stop and push across.' What do you do? You start pushing across. Imagery. He also teaches by feeling. I can feel something he said in my mind. There was one time I was wrestling him and he kept on tripping me. I'd have a two-on-one Russian on him, take it off and then I'd have him right in front of me. Then I was ready to shoot on him. Then the next thing I'd know I'd be on my butt because he had tripped me. So he kept on telling me, he kept on telling me, he kept on telling me that I didn't understand. Well, finally, I said, 'The heck with it.' But he said, 'Do it!' And he did it again to me. And I'd say, 'Okay, do it again.' As he was doing it he started to explain where he was pushing and how he was pushing. I started feeling what he was doing. You know, he explained it to me first. Then he just showed me what he was doing, and after a time I got it.

This may sound weird, but I believe when he gets really tired that psychs him up. When he gets tired he gets more energy and he wants to wrestle harder. It sounds weird, but the more I watch the man, the more I think that's the case.

*"I like to fish for walleye. It's the best fish to eat. It's not an unbelievable fighter, but it's kind of a trophy fish. It's one of the hardest fish to catch. You have to know their habits, daily."*

– Dan Gable

Dan Gable, fisherman.

# Eleven
## Days Spent Fishing

**J**on Marks, Iowa's former wrestling recruiter, is a storyteller. He believes in working hard and playing hard. There was once more time to fish on the Mississippi River at the Gables' family cabin. That was before six straight national championships at Iowa, though, and before people began asking for more and more of Gable's time in the summer, time he and Marks would usually have spent fishing for walleye.

Dan loves walleye. That's what he fishes for, boy. He's got one of those boats. What do you call them? Oh, yeah, a John boat. It's kind of a flat-bottomed boat, you know. He's got all the little gadgets that tell you how deep the water is, the temperature of the water and how deep you're supposed to be fishing in it. He knows the backwater. He knows it. You can get lost in there pretty easy because there's so much backwater up there.

Sometimes we start out at 4:30 in the morning and we'll be back by 11. We're out there for four or five hours at a time. There are times when we've gone out there and it's raining or cold. But, you know, with Dan you just sit around and it's fun. But if we aren't catching any fish, we don't just sit there. We'll move to another place. And he won't fish a place out, either. Not Dan! He'll catch a few and move on to another place, you know. When he catches those walleyes, he sticks his tongue out the side of his mouth. He gets excited, you know. When you catch something, he gets even more excited. It's like this: you're moving in the boat, always moving, like dragging, you know, and the first couple of times you've got something you don't know if you do or don't. You're pulling something in. And he says, 'Oh, hey, you've got a big one! Don't lose it!' You know, I don't know if I do or don't, but he says I do. Oh, but he gets excited. 'You've got a big 'ol wall-i-ga-tor!' he's screaming at you.

* * *

People tell Gable he ought to try deep-sea fishing, and he thinks he would like to do that, but then he figures he would miss the people who live along the Mississippi River. "They aren't the same kind of people as those who live along the Pacific or Atlantic oceans," he says. "River people aren't businessmen and they don't mind if you drink a beer or two, three or four, get drunk even." Gable says he couldn't get too rambunctious in downtown Iowa City, not without a lot of talk. But up at his family's cabin, near Lansing, Iowa, Gable can drink beer, fish and raise hell, if he wants. He likes knowing that.

Gable on fishing:

> I like to fish for walleye. It's the best fish to eat. It's not an unbelievable fighter, but it's kind of a trophy fish. It's one of the hardest fish to catch. You have to know their habits, daily. You never know where they're going to be. The challenge, the challenge, they're an unbelievable challenge. You've got to know where to find them. They go in schools and stay right in a spot together. Once you find them, there are thousands of them right in that one spot. If you find one walleye, mark the spot. If you go another hundred yards, you might not find one. But go back to that same spot and they're going to be all over.
> You know, I never was a walleye fisherman until I started coaching. I had never caught walleyes, except for when I went fishing up in Canada. That's the only fish up there to catch, walleyes and northerns. Comparing fishing for walleye to wrestling is pretty easy. When I was wrestling myself, it was pretty easy for me to be good. I knew what the hell to do. Winning was easy. It was like going out and fishing for bullheads. I like to fish for bullheads, but it's so simple.

You can drop your bobber and catch a thousand bullheads, if you want. When I became a coach, it wasn't that easy for me because I was beginning to deal with other people. It's much more of a challenge. It's so much harder to figure out. I'm dealing with so many people. And I'm dealing with their goals and not mine. And because of that I put more emphasis on achieving the same more difficult goals in fishing.

I love to take other people out. I can go out and just be the guide. It's like wrestling. People are so proud of it when they win. It's the same thing. They're so proud when they catch a fish. I'm happy because I'm the one who did it for them. Like I said, I can feel it when they catch walleye. It's like being the coach. It really doesn't mean that much to me, but I get satisfaction out of seeing it mean something to somebody else. So I'm the guide. If they catch fish, I feel great.

"And there would be this little red-headed guy sitting over there who just didn't look that tough."

— Bob Siddens

Iowa State coach Harold Nichols.

# Twelve
## Coaches

**B**ob Siddens, Gable's high school coach, first saw Dan wrestle when the youngster was in junior high. When Siddens is asked about Gable, he answers, "You have religious fanatics, and you have wrestling fanatics. Dan Gable was just a fanatic."

Siddens has retired as wrestling coach at Waterloo West High School, following 28 years in which he won 11 state team titles, finished second eight times and third three times. He enjoyed one string of 88 straight dual meet victories and coached his wrestlers to 58 individual state titles, including three by Gable. His high school career coaching record is 327-26-3. Siddens remains the athletic director at West High.

> The thing is that I don't have so many funny stories about Dan because he was so serious all of the time. The fun stories were just winning. His philosophy, my philosophy, was that you don't have fun unless you win. But, you know, he didn't look like he had that mental type of toughness to him. When somebody would come to the wrestling room, when Dan was a sophomore or junior, they would wonder where Dan Gable was. I'd say, 'That little guy sitting over there in the corner.' And there would be this little red-headed guy sitting over there who just didn't look that tough.

\* \* \*

Harold Nichols was Gable's wrestling coach at Iowa State. He is now coaching against Gable. Approached on a winter night, following a Hawkeye victory over his Cyclones in Ames, Nichols was asked, "What is the one thing that stands out in your mind when you think about Dan Gable?" Nichols answers with two words: "His intensity."

> He was like any other freshman I recruited, but he was determined, and he had goals to fulfill, and he

prepared himself for it. He got himself in superior condition by doing a lot of weight training, his way, by use of ankle and arm weights. None of the other wrestlers did that. Coordination-wise, there were a lot of people with better coordination, but as far as the goals he set for himself, he really worked at them.

I know what his motivation was. It was to fill a gap, as far as his parents were concerned. I think it's been said by himself at one time, but it's something I've suspected for years. He had a sister who was killed. I think he was trying to fill a void for his parents.

That last match he lost wasn't the only match he lost. He lost early in freestyle competition. But in that last match, really, I felt that there were some bad officiating calls. I know when he himself looked over at the scoreboard he felt helpless. I tried to get him going and at least finish it up as best as possible. I don't recall what I said to him afterwards. I just shook his hand. It was one of those things. It didn't weigh on me. I think his behavior, as much as anything, in going to the victory stand afterward was pretty exemplary.

And he got a bigger hand, a bigger ovation, than Owings did. I had a lot of pride that he was man enough, had enough character, to act that way.

*"Everybody feels they have to cheat to get somewhere. If the others just worked hard, they could be winners, too. That's what upsets him the most and makes him want to get out of it."*

– Kathy Gable

Dan Gable turns an opponent on his way to the Olympic Gold Medal in the 1972 Games in Munich.

# Thirteen

# Dan Gable: Legend and Husband

**K**athy Gable, Dan's wife, won't be going on as many Hawkeye wrestling trips as she has in the past, but she'll always make the national meet. No way she'll miss the national meet. But, otherwise, Kathy will be staying at home because their oldest daughter, Jenni, has started school.

Kathy first went out with Dan a few months after the 1972 Olympics. Their first date, on a June night, was a movie – *The Sound of Music*. They became engaged at Christmas time and were married the following spring. "No straight-out proposal," she says, "we just talked it over at a bar one night, and that was that."

> I remember watching Dan come home from the Olympics. We were to have a big celebration for him at an auditorium in Waterloo. His plane was supposed to be there at 8 o'clock, but it was delayed. He didn't get in until 2 a.m. But me and a bunch of girls waited. A few cheerleaders stayed and some band members. We all went over to a friend's house. We stayed up all night. I knew him well enough to do that kind of stuff.
>
> He was a pretty big celebrity when he came home from the Olympics. I remember he came home on a Thursday night. The next night he went to a football game. Waterloo Columbus was playing West High. They made the mistake of announcing he was at the game, and all these little kids started chasing him for his autograph. He looked real funny when he started running away from them. But they kept right up with him.
>
> It's not a hard life for me, being his wife. I don't feel like I'm different from anybody else. We don't live any kind of outlandish life. We live like normal people, in a house in Coralville.
>
> What will he do next? He thinks he's going to get out of coaching, but I say there's no way he will be

able to live without coaching. For one thing, he couldn't do it financially right now. Also, I just don't think he could really leave coaching. At least, he couldn't get out of it right now.

I think he's tired of fighting with the other schools. It makes him so mad. Everybody feels they have to cheat to get somewhere. If the others just worked hard, they could be winners, too. That's what upsets him the most and makes him want to get out of it.

Sometimes he says he'd move up to the river and fish. There's no way I'd move up to the Mississippi River and fish. I'm a fisherman, but not forever. The only thing I think he could do is endorse products, like he does now. He would have to stay in some kind of physical fitness thing. Something that we've talked about is that he'd like to build a camp on some land we bought. In the summer, he could bring in 40 or 50 kids a week and he could personally work with them. He wouldn't have to hire other people to work with him. And I could do the cooking.

I think that if he really had his way, he would quit coaching his U.S.A. teams in the off-season. I think he would like to get out of it, but I've kind of kept him in there. I really want him to push this one last time (the '84 Olympics). He owes it to himself and he owes it to some of these wrestlers.

*"Leaders are made. They are not born, and they are made just like anything else is made in this country — by hard effort."*

— Vince Lombardi

Dan Gable and assistant coach Mark Johnson at matside.

# Fourteen

# Office Hours

**D**an Gable sits in his office, doodling on a desktop calendar pad. He's talking on his black and gold telephone, talking business. He's doodling another rectangle around another day of another month, scribbling from the bottom of the page to the top. Those last empty squares, those squares past the 31st, are shaded almost to the borders. Sometimes he doodles in ink—red, black, blue. Sometimes he scribbles with a pencil. A lot of times he draws arrows, pointing to the few words written on the pad. One targeted word is "Oklahoma." Could he be wondering how to beat the Okies? Could he be considering a career move? Rumors are heard that Oklahoma State would like to hire him away from Iowa to coach the Cowboys, winners of 27 national wrestling titles, 20 more than any other school. Gable has won the last five. Because he has five national champions back to wrestle this year, the 1982-83 school year, fans expect him to make it six straight. Another wrestling season is hours away. It's early December. He's doodling on October. Whatever happened to November?

Three phone calls later, still talking business, Gable pushes his pencil into the electric sharpener, spinning the lead into another point. On his desk is a schedule for the upcoming season. On the wall in front of him is a photo full of wrestling buddies, their hands holding beers raised high, toasting some past, but not forgotten, moment. On another part of the wall are a pair of aging Iowa bumper stickers, slogans from three seasons ago.

He's stashed cardboard boxes all around him. Some are under his desk, some are behind him, full of caps from advertisers—Amana Refrigeration, Tiger shoes, Mountain Dew. There are 14, maybe 16, caps in all. He never wears them. In another box, waiting for shelves and tacks, are trophies and plaques. Two boxes are empty.

Reaching higher and higher, like stepping stones, from desktop to the ceiling, are coaching creeds. The message on his desk, burned into a wooden map of Iowa, reads: "Too good to be No. 2." At eye-level, taped to the wall is a cartoon drawing, a girl saying: "Bring out all the best in you." Above that cartoon, Vince Lombardi quotations smack harder. Two of Lombardi's thoughts are taped to the wall. They're both alike. Here's one: "Leaders are made. They are not born, and they are made just like anything else is made in this country—by hard effort." Above the windows are three personal prizes. The left one says, "To the Super Coaches." It's from the 1975-79 wrestlers. The middle one is a thank you from Mike DeAnna, a wrestler who won four all-American honors at Iowa but never a national championship. DeAnna has engraved this thought: "To Dan Gable—In appreciation for all you have done for me to help me achieve my goals." At right is a picture of Gable's two daughters, Jenni and Annie, one of the four photos of them smiling at him in this office corner.

When the daughters visit their daddy at work, they reach into his lower right-hand desk drawer, the double-bottomed one that holds the Big Bird puzzle, the Donald Duck storybook, the dolls, the coloring books. On the bottom left is Gable's "daily needs" drawer, the one with window cleaner, instant tea, flight-wrapped peanuts, Cheez-it snack chips and Super Heroes cookies.

Facing him on his desk is a row of books. Some of their outer pages touch the partition that separates Gable from an assistant coach. One book title reads, *Strength Training for Football: The Penn State Way.* Another title reads, *Peak Performances: Mental Game Plans for Maximizing Your Athletic Potential.* Mixed among the books are telephone directories: a city telephone book, a college student directory, a national coaches' directory. But Gable never looks up one number—wife Kathy and home. Sometimes he calls her just to talk. Sometimes they talk about the 26 wooded acres of land they own. Sometimes he talks about his vegetable garden, his apple orchard, his raspberry bushes, his grape vines. Sometimes, he talks about going into forestry.

The Gable family. Seated on Dan's lap are Jenni (left) and Annie. Kathy holds Molly. Seated above Dan are his parents, Mack and Kate.

# Fifteen

# An Ending—Because All Books Have To Have One

**D**an Gable leans over the kitchen table in his Coralville home. Jennifer, his 6-year-old daughter, sits in a chair. He teases her as she eats ice cream.

"Jennifer, do you know what I do?"
"Yes."
"Don't look away, Jennifer. What do I do?"
"Coach. Daddy coaches."
"What do I coach? Do I coach football?"
"No."
"What then?"
"Wrestling."
"And do you know where I went to school?"
"Boo, Iowa State."
"Hey, I went to school there. I wrestled there."
"Boo, Iowa State."
"Jennifer, who do you cheer for when Daddy's coaching?"
"Go Hawks!"

# Steve Holland

# Talkin' Dan Gable

"Never before have I read a book concerning myself where I learned so much about my personal qualities. The piece seems so true and realistic. This work has given me a more thorough understanding of myself. It personally has moved me on several occasions to the point of bringing tears to my eyes."

— Olympic wrestling coach and Olympic champion Dan Gable

## Order **Talkin' Dan Gable** for a friend

---

Send check or money order to:

Talkin' Dan Gable
Box 2104
Iowa City, IA 52244

Enclosed is $_____ for _____ copies of Talkin' Dan Gable at $7.95 each.

Limerick Publications

Name _____
Address _____
City _____ State _____ Zip Code

Include $1.50 per book for postage and handling.
Allow 3 weeks for delivery.

---

Send check or money order to:

Talkin' Dan Gable
Box 2104
Iowa City, IA 52244

Enclosed is $_____ for _____ copies of Talkin' Dan Gable at $7.95 each.

Limerick Publications

Name _____
Address _____
City _____ State _____ Zip Code

Include $1.50 per book for postage and handling.
Allow 3 weeks for delivery.

---

Send check or money order to:

Talkin' Dan Gable
Box 2104
Iowa City, IA 52244

Enclosed is $_____ for _____ copies of Talkin' Dan Gable at $7.95 each.

Limerick Publications

Name _____
Address _____
City _____ State _____ Zip Code

Include $1.50 per book for postage and handling.
Allow 3 weeks for delivery.

# Also available from Limerick Publications

Send your friends the cover of **Talkin' Dan Gable** reproduced on color postcards. Available in packets of 10 for $3.

---

Send check or money order to:

Talkin' Dan Gable
Box 2104
Iowa City, IA 52244

Limerick Publications

Name _____
Address _____
City      State      Zip Code

Enclosed is $_____ for _____ packets of Talkin' Dan Gable postcards at $3 per packet of ten.

---

Send check or money order to:

Talkin' Dan Gable
Box 2104
Iowa City, IA 52244

Limerick Publications

Name _____
Address _____
City      State      Zip Code

Enclosed is $_____ for _____ packets of Talkin' Dan Gable postcards at $3 per packet of ten.

---

Send check or money order to:

Talkin' Dan Gable
Box 2104
Iowa City, IA 52244

Limerick Publications

Name _____
Address _____
City      State      Zip Code

Enclosed is $_____ for _____ packets of Talkin' Dan Gable postcards at $3 per packet of ten.